HBJ Mathematics

Year 6

Daphne Kerslake
Leone Burton
Richard Harvey
Lilian Street
Angela Walsh

Collins Educational

An imprint of HarperCollinsPublishers

First published in 1992 by Harcourt Brace Jovanovich Ltd

This edition published in 1993 by Collins Educational
An imprint of HarperCollins*Publishers*
77–85 Fulham Palace Road
London W6 8JB

Printed and bound in Great Britain by Cambus Litho, East Kilbride

ISBN 0 00 300506 2

Contents

Acknowledgements

Trialling teachers: Year 6

Athersley South Junior School, Barnsley
Mrs K. Bevis
Mrs N. Bissell
Mrs S. Haney
Mr M. Smith
Ms R. Twist

Bareham Primary School, Wembley
Mrs Y.E. Morrell
Mr J.M. Redpath

Bentley V C Primary School, Ipswich
Mrs M.R. Eccles

Bramley Sunnyside Junior School, Rotherham
Mrs S. Foster

Cayley J M I School, London
Ms D. Harvey

Claydon County Primary School, Ipswich
Miss S. Copson

Commonswood J M I School, Welwyn Garden City
Mrs S. Hart
Mr R.W. Harris

Cravenwood Primary School, Manchester
Mrs I. Overfield

Elmwood County Primary School, Manchester
Miss M. Meadows
Mrs E.Turner

Glan-Yr-Afon Junior School, Cardiff
Ms G. May

Grafton Primary School, London
Ms D. Toth

Handsworth Primary School, London
Miss K. Weston

Hargrave Park Primary School, London
Ms E.A. Weir

Haroldswick Primary School, Shetland
Ms E. Black

Hutton C E V C Primary School, Hutton
Mrs J. Utteridge

Hyde Park Junior School, Plymouth
Mr M.J. Kimpton

Lever Edge County Primary School, Bolton
Ms K. Cresswell

Marown School, Glen Vine, Isle of Man
Ms J. Pontée

May Park Primary School, Bristol
Mr J. Trimble

Pocklington County Junior School, York
Mr D.N. Carr

Ramridge Junior School, Luton
Mr R. Oglesby
Mr J. Seaton
Mr R. Teague

Rettendon C P School, Chelmsford
Miss S. Cage

St Albans Primary School, Newcastle
Mr M. Donnelly

St Edward's R C Primary School, London
Mr K.D. Beckwith

St Marks First and Middle School, Hanwell
Mrs J. Posthumus

St Margaret's-at-Cliffe C P School, Dover
Ms C. Taylor

Saltash Junior School, Saltash
Mr D.H. Jones
Mr B. Lean
Ms H.T. Simmill

Scole C E Primary School, Diss
Mr K.J. Abbott

Shakerley C E J & I School, Manchester
Mrs A. Ladd

Westfields Primary School, London
Mr A.J. King
Mrs A. Pickering

Westwood County Primary School, Oldham
Mr R. Knight

All the teachers named above are thanked for their willingness to use and comment on pre-publication versions of the books. Their comments proved invaluable in the development of this programme. Many thanks are due also to all the teachers' assistants and children who participated in the trialling.

We would also like to thank the children, staff and head teachers of Avondale Park Primary School, London, and Fox Primary School, London, and W.H. Smith of Orpington, Kent, for helping us with the photographs.

Marmite is a registered trademark of CPC International Inc, reproduced by kind permission of CPC (UK) Ltd. Photograph of *Smarties* cartons by permission of Société des Produits Nestlé SA, Vevey, Switzerland.

Literacy consultant—Chris Lutrario

Illustrations—Kathy Baxendale, John Plumb and DP Press

Design and cover—Neil Adams at DP Press

Photographs—Garry Fry Stills Photography and Daphne Kerslake, with Janice English, Julie English, Keith Silk, Lilian Street and Sheila White

Change

Make up some multiplications that use all four of these numerals in any arrangement.

What is the biggest answer you can get?

Try it with four different starting numerals.

Write about what you find out.

635 × 4
53 × 46
3 × 564

 ## Changing numbers

Look at this number pattern.
Discuss the patterns that go along the rows and down the columns.

1	3	5	7	9
2	6	10	14	18
4	12	20	28	36
8	24	40	56	72

Continue each row and column.

Ask yourselves some questions like:

Would every number appear somewhere in the pattern?

Where is 1000?

Does any number appear more than once?

If you multiply any two numbers in the top row, you get another number in the top row. Does this happen with other rows or columns?

Changing size

Collect some packets or jars that are
the same shape but different sizes.

How do their sizes compare?

Are they full to the top when you buy them?

Are the larger sizes better value for money?
How did you work it out?

Changing views

Make some three-dimensional models out of straws.
Choose one and look at it from different positions.

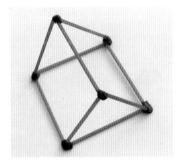 

Draw exactly what you see.
Exchange your drawings with someone else and ask them to work
out what shape you used.

What shadows can you make by hanging up your model against
the light? Draw what you see.

Anthony chose some numbers.

17 23 72
486 181 4 55

He used his calculator to
multiply each number by 0.9.

Eman multiplied the same
numbers by 1.1.
Anthony said his numbers
got smaller.
Eman said hers got bigger.
Do you agree?

Try multiplying by 0.95 or 1.05.
Try some other numbers close to 1.

Small changes in turns

This LOGO program draws a square.

```
TO SQUARE
FD 100 RT 90
SQUARE
END
```

Try it. It goes on drawing the same square over and over again until you press ESCAPE.

Now make a new program with a small change in the angle.
Try 89° or 91° instead of 90°. What happens this time?

Try some more angle changes.

Start with a triangle and see what happens.

How many small white triangles
are there in this triangle?

How many small blue triangles?

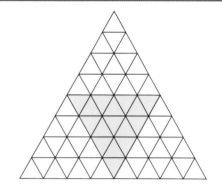

How are these two patterns made?

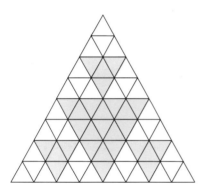
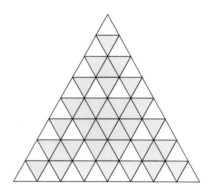

What fraction of the triangle is coloured blue each time?

Will there be as much as $\frac{3}{4}$ of the triangle
coloured blue when this pattern is
completed?

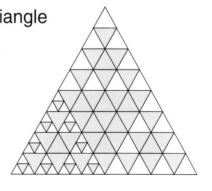

Make a similar pattern starting with a bigger triangle. You could use
32 or 64 triangles like this △ along the base. What is the
biggest fraction of the triangle you coloured in?

Changing groups

Sarah used 26 sticks to make some squares and some triangles.

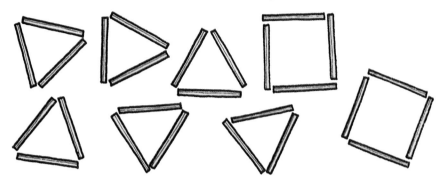

Find another way of arranging all 26 sticks to make squares and triangles.

Sarah says there are three different ways of making squares and triangles using exactly 35 sticks, and four different ways if she uses 46 sticks.

Do you agree?

Find some other numbers of sticks that can be made into squares and triangles in more than one way.

Challenge some other people with your examples.

Changing shapes

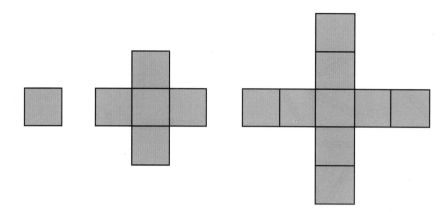

How many squares are there in each pattern?

How many will there be in the next pattern?

Continue these patterns so that they get bigger and bigger.

How many squares will there be in the 10th pattern? in the 15th? in the 100th?

How did you work it out?

Make some more patterns of your own and make up some similar questions to answer.

Chains of numbers

Leon chose the number  34 . He used the rule:

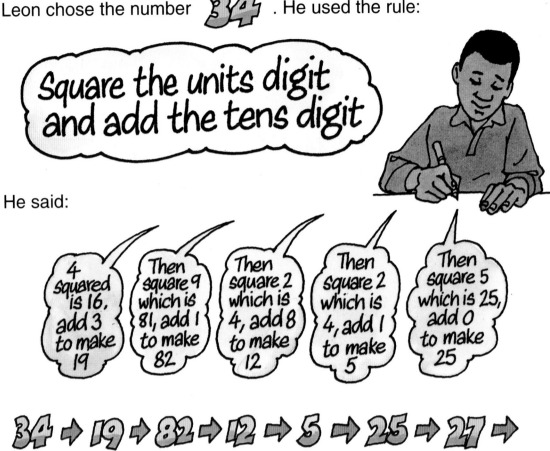

Square the units digit and add the tens digit

He said:

4 squared is 16, add 3 to make 19

Then square 9 which is 81, add 1 to make 82

Then square 2 which is 4, add 8 to make 12

Then square 2 which is 4, add 1 to make 5

Then square 5 which is 25, add 0 to make 25

34 → 19 → 82 → 12 → 5 → 25 → 27 →

Try some other starting numbers and use Leon's rule.
What happens?

Make a picture to show all your number chains.

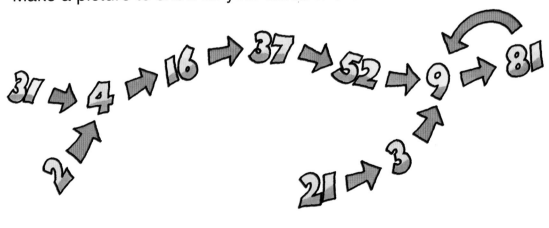

31 → 4 → 16 → 37 → 52 → 9 → 81

2 → 4

21 → 3 → 9

13

Getting bigger

Find out about the sizes of photographs and their enlargements.

How much bigger are the enlargements?

Find out about A4, A3 and A2 paper sizes.

How much bigger are the bigger sheets?
How many of the smaller sheets make the larger ones?
What size is A5?
How small a piece of paper can you make in this set?

Make some enlargements using an overhead projector if you have one.

Bigger and bigger cubes

Make a set of open paper cubes with
sides of 1 centimetre, 2 centimetres,
3 centimetres and 4 centimetres.

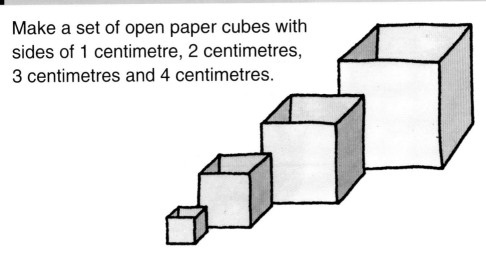

How many centimetre cubes will fit into each?
How many would fit in the next size up? and the next?

How many square centimetres of paper
are used to make each cube?

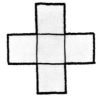

Display your results. You could make a table or draw a graph.

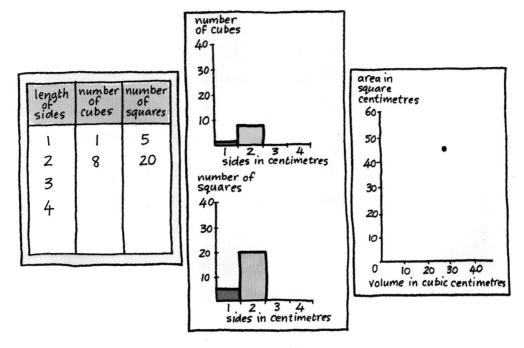

length of sides	number of cubes	number of squares
1	1	5
2	8	20
3		
4		

15

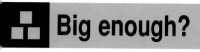

The instructions for a knitting pattern are:

Row 1: repeat 4 times (knit 6 blue, knit 6 green).

Row 2: repeat 4 times (knit 6 green, knit 6 blue).

Repeat these two rows.

Row 5: repeat 4 times (knit 6 green, knit 6 blue).

Row 6: repeat 4 times (knit 6 blue, knit 6 green).

Repeat these two rows.

Repeat these 8 rows 4 more times.

Draw on squared paper what the pattern will look like.

The tension is: 16 stitches to 10 cm
                    20 rows to 10 cm

How big will the knitting be?

Write the instructions for a bigger or smaller piece of knitting.

Different views

These are different views of the same shape made out of six cubes.

Make a shape of your own and decide how to draw different views of it.

Exchange your drawings with other people. Can they make your shape?

Janine, Rahsia, Emma and David all started with a shape like this:

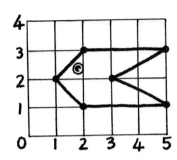

The coordinates of
the points are:
(1,2) (2,3) (5,3) (3,2) (5,1) (2,1)

Janine changed the picture by adding 2 to the first number of each pair of numbers. Emma doubled both numbers of the pair. Rahsia subtracted 1 from the second number of the pair. David doubled the first number of the pair and halved the second.

Who drew which shape?

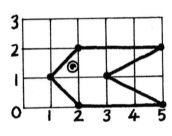

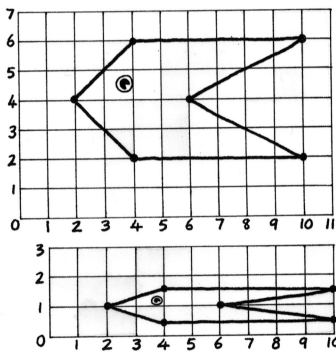

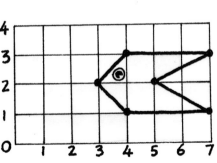

Make up a shape of your own and change the coordinates.
Exchange them with each other and work out the rules for changing the shapes.

Changing points

Lee drew this shape on a grid:

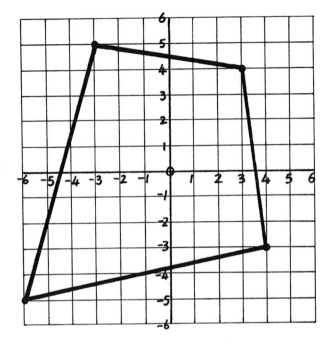

He gave Lorraine the points as (3,4) (4,–3) (–6,–5) (–3,5).

He asked her to add 6 to the first number of each pair and draw the new shape. How is Lorraine's shape different from Lee's shape?

Draw a shape on a grid.
Make up some rules for changing the coordinates. You could double both numbers, or double one and halve the other.

Try some other shapes.

Weather report

True or false?

s it true that…

..six is the hardest to get?

…girls are taller than boys?

..mental arithmetic is fastest?

…bricks are always laid in this pattern?

Stamps for letters

Is it true that any amount can be made using combinations of 3p and 5p stamps only? You can use as many of each as you like.

What about other pairs of stamps?

 # Car box

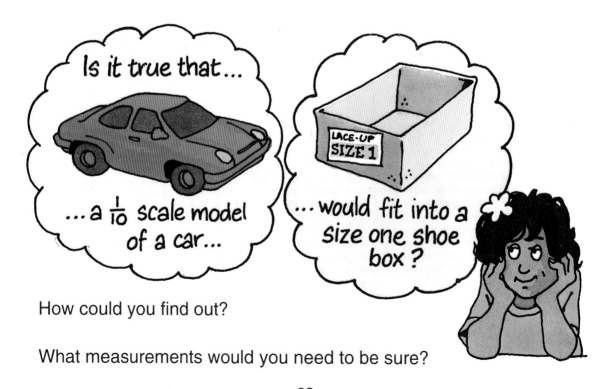

Is it true that... ...a $\frac{1}{10}$ scale model of a car...

...would fit into a size one shoe box?

How could you find out?

What measurements would you need to be sure?

About people

Is it true that the height of a person is the same as three times the distance round their head?

Playing *Nim*

This is a game for two players. You will need 15 counters.
Put the counters in a pile. Take turns to remove 1, 2 or 3 counters from the pile. The player who takes the last counter is the winner.

Is it true that the first player to go always wins?
What strategy should the first player use?

Is it true that 2078 is the answer to all these questions?

$4099 - 2021$

$6235 \div 3$

$$\begin{array}{r} 96 \\ 273 \\ 1094 \\ 625 + \\ \hline \\ \hline \end{array}$$

$2000 + 70 + 8$

62×34

$4079 \div 2$

$$\begin{array}{r} 978 \\ 1100 + \\ \hline \\ \hline \end{array}$$

$4156 \div 20$

$2078000 \div 100$

207.8×10

Which do you need to check?

Make up some questions of your own that have the answer 2078.

Use a die to enter numbers into a grid like this:

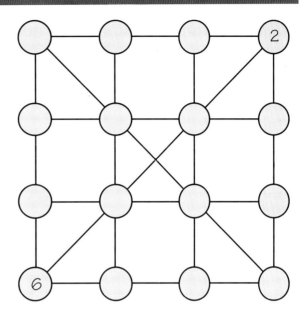

Continue until all the spaces are full.

Pick a straight line of four numbers from your grid. Use mathematical signs to combine the numbers, keeping them in order, to give an answer as near to 12 as possible.

Your score is the difference between your number and 12.

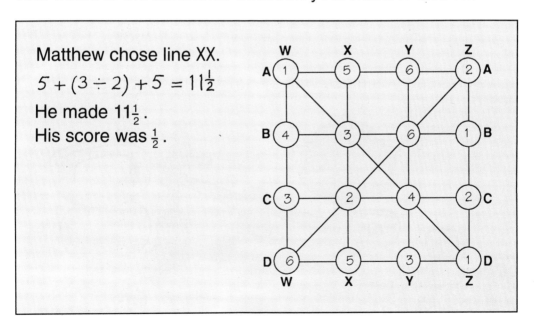

Matthew chose line XX.

$$5 + (3 \div 2) + 5 = 11\tfrac{1}{2}$$

He made $11\tfrac{1}{2}$.
His score was $\tfrac{1}{2}$.

Take turns to do this until all ten lines are used up. Add up your scores. The person with the smallest total is the winner.

These weights are 1 ounce, 2 ounces, 4 ounces, 8 ounces and 16 ounces (1 lb).

Is it true that you could use these weights to weigh any item up to 31 ounces?

If you added a 32 ounce weight what weights could you make?

What weights can you make with these? What weights can't you make?

Will it fit?

Use 5 cubes to make this shape:

Show that it can fit exactly
into each hole in
this posting box.

Are there any other holes into which it will fit exactly?

Make one shape to fit
these three holes
exactly:

Make one shape for
these three holes:

Invent some more of these.

Boxing clever

Draw an accurate net for an
open box which is a
10 cm cube.

What area of card will you need to make it?

Make the box. What is its volume?

Repeat this for different sized boxes.
Estimate your answers first.

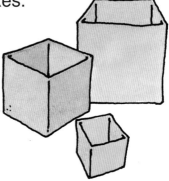

If you know the dimensions of a cube…

  …is it true that you can work out the area of card you will need
  to make it?

  …is it true that you can find the volume of the completed box?

Try the same activity with a
different shaped box.

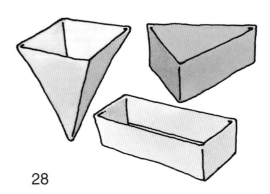

Predicting volumes

Find a marble and a cricket ball and measure their diameters.

Now find their volumes.

Is it true that if you know the diameter of any ball you can predict its volume?

Diameter	Volume
2 cm	4.5 cc
4 cm	33 cc
6 cm	113.5 cc
8 cm	270 cc
10 cm	520 cc
12 cm	903 cc

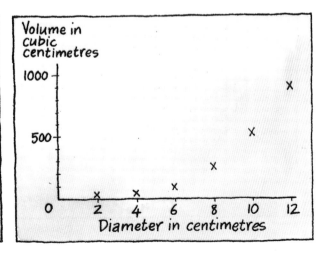

What if you use cubes instead of spheres?

Legs and running

Is it true that the longer your legs the faster you can run?

Test it out for your group.

Marcus and his group recorded their findings like this:

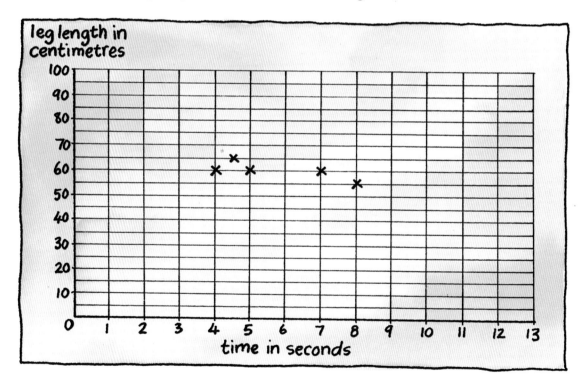

Add your results to the class scatter graph.

What information does the scatter graph give you?

Potatoes

Is it true that most potatoes weigh between 200 g and 300 g?

How many potatoes did you try?
Was that enough?

What else could you say if you used more potatoes?

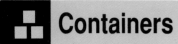

Containers

Is it true that the dimensions of a container are a good indication of what it will hold?

Compare some containers in your classroom.

Choose one container. Design another container which holds less but looks as though it holds more.

Bingo

This is a game for four players. You need will need two dice, one numbered 1, 2, 4, 6, 8, 12 and one numbered 2, 3, 4, 8, 9, 12.

You will also need some counters and each of you will need one of these cards:

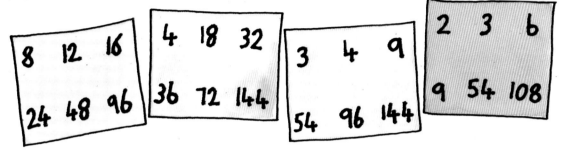

To play the game you take turns to throw two dice, multiply the scores and call out the answer. All the players cover that number if it is on their card. You win if you are the first one to cover all the numbers on your card.

I've got a 36 so I'll cross it off

Play the game several times. Is it true that one card is the winning card more often than the others?

Convince yourselves about the answer.

Even or odd?

You need a pack of playing cards with the picture cards removed, or four sets of cards numbered from 1 to 10.

Take turns to shuffle the cards and pick any two.

Multiply their numbers together and record whether the answer is an even number or an odd number. Decide how many times you will do this.

Is it true that you get more odd answers than even?

How many times do you think you should try the experiment?

Find a way to explain what you discovered.

Fair or unfair?

Use a game board like this to make up two games.

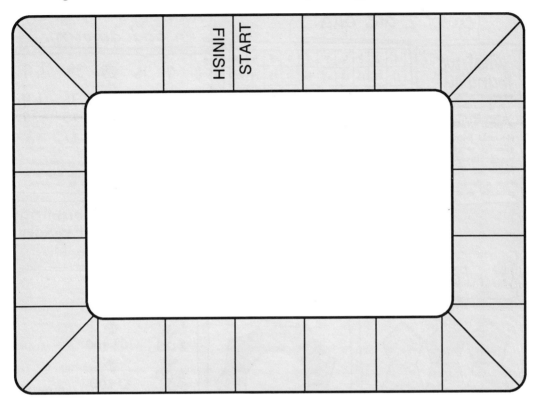

One game should be 'fair' so that every player has a fair chance of winning. The other should be 'unfair' so that one player is more likely to win than the others.

Try the games several times.
Convince yourselves that they work as you expect.

False or true?

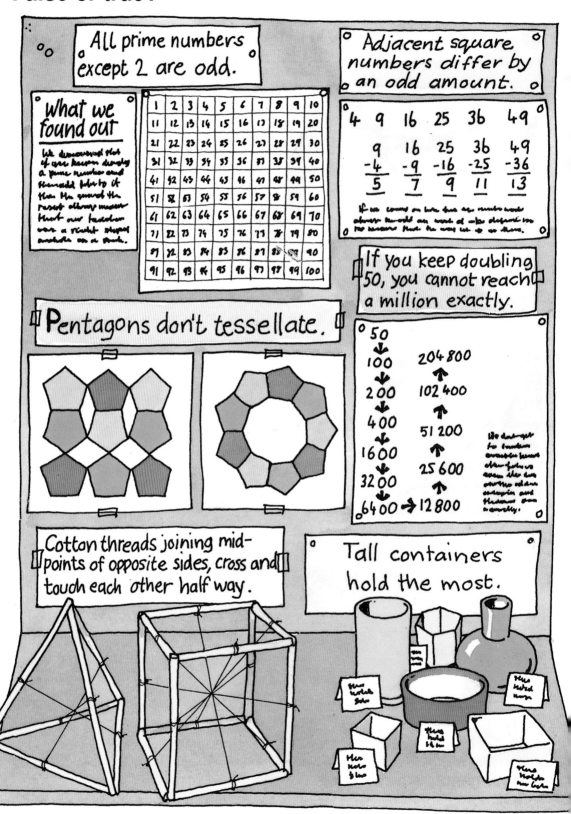

All prime numbers except 2 are odd.

Adjacent square numbers differ by an odd amount.

What we found out

We discovered that if you keep doubling a prime number and then add one to it then the answer always meant that our teacher was a right stupid article on a book.

1	2	3	4	5	6	7	8	9	10
11	12	13	14	15	16	17	18	19	20
21	22	23	24	25	26	27	28	29	30
31	32	33	34	35	36	37	38	39	40
41	42	43	44	45	46	47	48	49	50
51	52	53	54	55	56	57	58	59	60
61	62	63	64	65	66	67	68	69	70
71	72	73	74	75	76	77	78	79	80
81	82	83	84	85	86	87	88	89	90
91	92	93	94	95	96	97	98	99	100

4   9   16   25   36   49

$$9 - 4 = 5$$
$$16 - 9 = 7$$
$$25 - 16 = 9$$
$$36 - 25 = 11$$
$$49 - 36 = 13$$

If we count on here there are numbers which always hundred are made of odd adjacent too. We became that the way we do so them.

If you keep doubling 50, you cannot reach a million exactly.

50
↓
100
↓
200
↓
400
↓
1600
↓
3200
↓
6400 → 12 800

204 800
↑
102 400
↑
51 200
↑
25 600
↑
12 800

We don't get to two even when we even the two other column swappin and there are an everly.

Pentagons don't tessellate.

Cotton threads joining midpoints of opposite sides, cross and touch each other half way.

Tall containers hold the most.

Somewhere local

Choose somewhere local that you could visit.

What route would you take to get there from school? What places will you pass through? How will you travel?

What else will you need to think about?

Make a brochure about it for your travel agency.

Choose a country

Katie's group chose to collect information about France and organized a 'French Week' at the travel agency.

Choose a country for your group and decide what to tell people about it:

    hotels…
    places to visit…
    the climate…
    the food…
    how to get there…

Set up a data-base with information suitable for a travel agency.

Which holiday?

Where would you choose to go for a 2-week holiday?

Work out the cost of a 2-week holiday in that place for a family of four. What will you need to consider?

Tourist attractions

Which places in Britain do you think receive the most visitors?

Can you predict the top 6? Would one of them be the Houses of Parliament, for example?

When you have chosen six places, check the official information to find out if your predictions were correct.

How many people went to the most popular place? Visualize how many people this is. How does it compare with the number of people in your class, or in your school? How did you work this out?

Samira and Toni are working out the best way to go from Newtown to Braceford.

Car - 30 mph
How far? 45 miles

Train
leaves at 09.28
arrives at 10.12

Coach
leaves at 09.00
arrives at 10.45

How long will each journey take?

What place did you choose to visit in **Somewhere local?**

Find out about different ways of travelling to your destination.
Work out how long each would take.
What would be the best time to travel?

What does it cost?

Samira and Toni are working out the cost to travel from Newtown to Braceford.

Routes to Braceford

By car – 45 miles at 30 m p h
car uses 1 gallon
for 30 miles

By train – £5.50 standard fare
£4.30 excursion fare
(after 9.30)

By coach – £3.20 return

What does each journey cost?

Which is the cheapest?

What place did you choose to visit in **Somewhere local?**

Work out the cost of different ways of getting there.

Which is the cheapest way to travel?

Making a decision

Look at your information about travelling to the place you have chosen.

Compare costs and compare journey times. Think about how easy and how enjoyable the journeys are.

Decide on your best way to go and why.

Which hotel?

People on this tour can choose their hotel. How could they decide which would be the cheapest and which would be the most expensive?

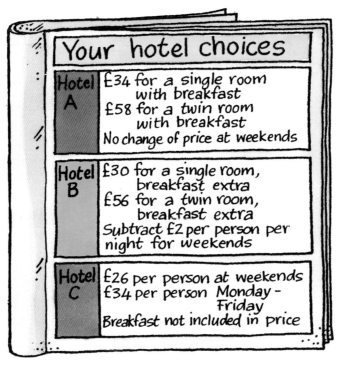

Your hotel choices

Hotel A	£34 for a single room with breakfast
	£58 for a twin room with breakfast
	No change of price at weekends

Hotel B	£30 for a single room, breakfast extra
	£56 for a twin room, breakfast extra
	Subtract £2 per person per night for weekends

Hotel C	£26 per person at weekends
	£34 per person Monday – Friday
	Breakfast not included in price

Look at the hotel choices and prices on your data-base and work out the different costs.

Which hotels would you recommend to customers and why?

What questions might customers ask you about the country you have chosen?

Use your data-base to help you answer the questions, adding to it if necessary.

Check that customers could now use the data-base themselves to answer their queries.

Passports

People travelling sometimes need a passport. A passport gives information about you to other people.

You are soon to travel to secondary school. Decide what to put in a mathematical passport that you could take with you.

It could show what you like best in mathematics, your favourite numbers, what you know and anything else you think is important.

What will we pack?

What information does your holiday brochure give you about the weather at the place you chose for your holiday? What questions will you need to ask about your holiday destination to help you decide what to pack?

Try to find out some of the answers.
How much space will your things need?

If you were going on an aeroplane, what would be the maximum weight of luggage you could take?

Find out how heavy this feels and what it might look like.

Departure times

Where does your holiday start from?

What time will you need to leave home to be sure to arrive in time to begin your holiday?

What do you need to think about in making your decision?

Brian's holiday starts at Gatwick.
They have to be there to check in at 11.30.

What time do you think they should catch a train at Redwick?

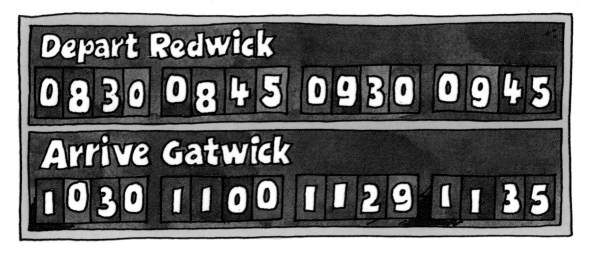

How much money?

How much money will you need to take on holiday?

Think about the things that you will have to pay for that are not included in the holiday.

How much are you likely to need each day for food? travel? fun?

How will you work out how much to take?

If your holiday is abroad, find out about the local currency. Find out about the coins and notes you will be using.

A tourist guide

Choose one of the most popular places for visitors and find out as much information as you can about it.

Think about what information would be helpful for a visitor and how you will present it.

Make a tourist guide about it for your travel agency.

How do we get there?

Make a map to show visitors how to get to your chosen place.

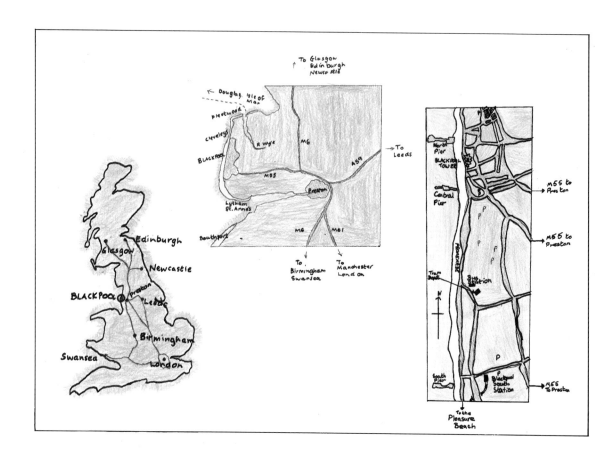

How many road routes are there?

Is it possible to reach it by rail or coach without having to walk too far?

What information would visitors need to help them decide how to get there?

What about visitors from abroad? How would they get there from an airport or ferry terminal?

Different ways of paying

How much does it cost to visit your tourist attraction?

Find out what this would be in different currencies.

Choose one foreign currency and find out all you can about it.
Write an information sheet about it for your travel agency.

You could draw a conversion graph.

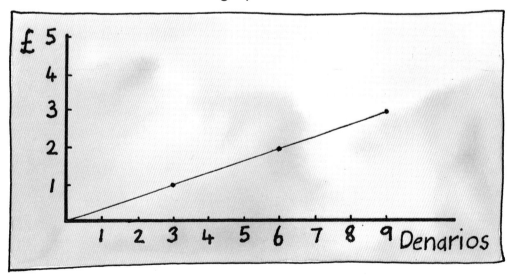

Come to our travel agency!

Closer and closer

Attach one end of a piece of string to a solid object and tie a pencil to the other end. Stretch the string and make the pencil draw a path as it wraps round the object.

Try it with objects of other shapes.
What is the same about the drawings? What is different?

▲ Step patterns

To make the pattern, Kim walks in a straight line towards the door. After each step, she pauses and puts a counter on the floor by her feet. Ellen faces Kim and walks towards her. After every step she puts a counter by her feet and faces Kim again.

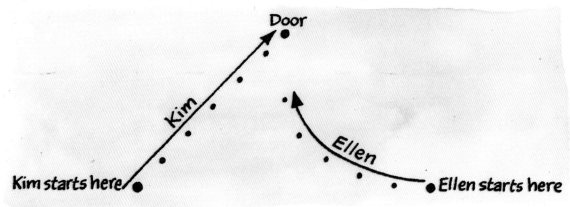

Try it for yourself and find out what happens.
What would happen if Kim turned around and walked back again?
What would happen if she walked in a circle?

Squaring up

A square has an area of 20 square centimetres. What is the length of each side?

What is the length of each side if the area of the square is 24 square centimetres?

What will you try next? How close can you get?

Where is it going?

Work out how to find more terms for this sequence:

$$1, 1, 2, 3, 5, 8, 13 \ldots$$

Look at this sequence:

$$\frac{1}{1}, \frac{2}{1}, \frac{3}{2}, \frac{5}{3} \ldots$$

Work out some more terms.

Sally wrote the sequence out again like this:

$$1, 2, 1\tfrac{1}{2} \text{ or } 1.5 \ldots$$

What do you notice?

What happens if she continues like this?

This is the beginning of
a 2, 3, 4 pattern:

The instructions are:

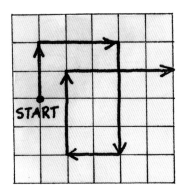

Forward 2
Right turn 90°
Forward 3
Right turn 90°
Forward 4
Right turn 90°

Continue repeating the sequence. What happens?

Try a 3, 4, 5 pattern.

Make some more patterns with three digits. Do you always get back to where you started? What else can you say about the patterns?

Here is the beginning of a 1, 2, 3, 1 pattern:

What happens if you continue it?

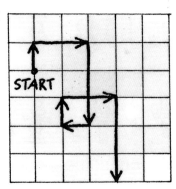

What does a 1, 3, 2, 1 pattern look like?

Try some more four-digit patterns. Which patterns make closed shapes? Which do not? Find some rules.

LOGO spirals

Here is one way of drawing a spiral with LOGO:

```
TO SQSPI
FD 80 RT 90
FD 70 RT 90
FD 60 RT 90
FD 50 RT 90
FD 40 RT 90
FD 30 RT 90
END
```

How close can you make the turtle get to the centre of the spiral? (You may need to adjust the forward distances to suit your version of LOGO.)

Another program is:

```
TO SQSPI :LENGTH
REPEAT 10 [FD :LENGTH RT 90 MAKE "LENGTH :LENGTH – 10]
END
```

Type SQSPI 100 or SQSPI 50 and see what happens.

Change the program so the turtle gets closer to the centre of the spiral.

Write a program that draws a hexagonal or an octagonal spiral.

57

Make a set of triangles from squares like these:

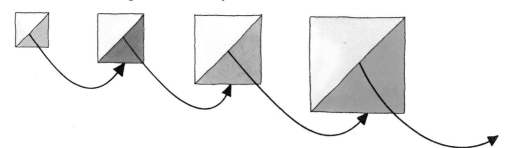

The diagonal of each square gives the length of the side of the next square in the sequence.

Cut out the triangles and stick them on centimetre squared paper to make a spiral that looks like this:

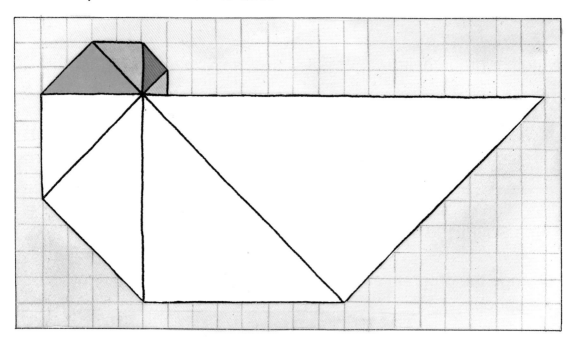

Measure the sides of all your triangles.
What do you notice about the lengths of sides along grid lines?
What do you notice about the other sides?

What do you notice about the areas of your triangles?

What other ways can you find of drawing spirals?

Curves of pursuit

Four children made up a dance. They each stood at the corner of a square, facing the person ahead of them.

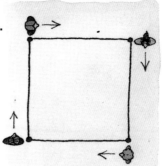

Each of them took one step forward. Then they looked to see where the person they were following had moved to. They set off in that direction and took another step forward.

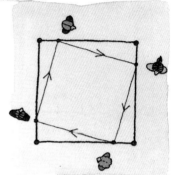

After they had done this several times, they made a pattern of their dance.

Work out how their pattern was made.

What pattern would they make if three people started at the corners of an equilateral triangle? What would happen if the triangle was not equilateral?

Try it with people starting at the corners of other shapes.

Middle point paths

Mandy, Nick and Jenny all set off from the same place. Mandy walked in one direction and Nick in another. Jenny walked between them and tried to keep exactly halfway between Mandy and Nick.

They marked where they were after each step by placing a counter on the floor by their feet.

They recorded their steps like this:

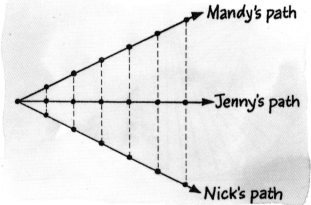

Try it for yourselves.

What happens if Mandy takes longer steps than Nick? or if she takes two steps to every one step of Nick's?

What happens if Nick walks in a straight line and Mandy walks in a square? or in a circle?

Rolling straight-sided shapes

This large box is being rolled about its red edges.

This is a diagram to show how the front face of the box moves.

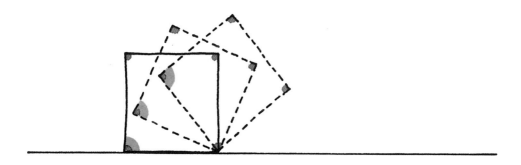

Cut out some squares and show the path the green corner traces. When will the green corner reach the ground again?

What happens if a triangle is rolled along a straight line? or a hexagon?

What happens if one square rolls around another square?

What numbers?

These are consecutive numbers:

3, 4, 5

23, 24, 25, 26

19, 20

Two consecutive numbers multiply to make 1406. What are they?

Two consecutive numbers multiply to make 3422. What are they?

Three consecutive numbers multiply to make 4896. What are they?

Three consecutive numbers multiply to make 97290. What are they?

Make up some more consecutive number questions.

What measurement?

Make some rectangles with an area of 24 squares.

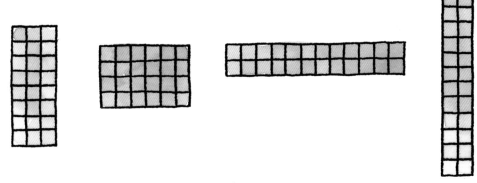

Here are some ways of representing information about the rectangles you have made.

Length	1	2	3	4	6	8	12	24
Width	24	12	8					

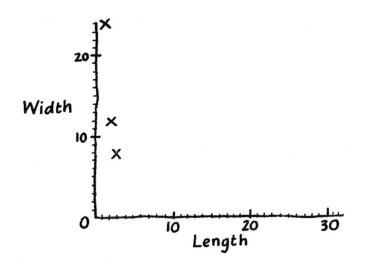

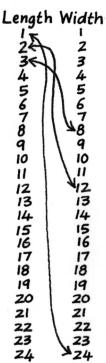

Which way will you choose?

Make some rectangles with an area of 36 square centimetres. Record your information in different ways.

How are your diagrams or graphs the same? How are they different?

All the way round

Jack and Kanchani found the perimeter and length of all their rectangles with an area of 24 square centimetres.

They plotted the information on a graph.

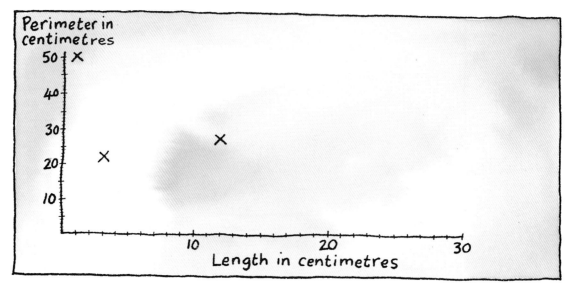

Find the perimeters of the rectangles with an area of 36 square centimetres that you made in **What measurement?**

Record the length and perimeter of each rectangle.

Draw a graph and plot all the information you have about your rectangles. Discuss the shape of the graph and write about it.

How far?

Freda wants to reach the edge of the pond, which is 32 metres away.

On Monday she jumps halfway, a distance of 16 metres.
On Tuesday she jumps half as far, a distance of 8 metres.
Every day after that she jumps half as far as the day before.

How far has she jumped by Saturday?

When will she reach the edge of the pond?

When shall I stop?

You will need two dice, each with three faces coloured red, two faces coloured blue and one face coloured yellow.

Decide who will play first. When it is your turn, you throw both dice.

You score like this:

Two reds	1 point
One red, one blue	2 points
Two blues	3 points
One red, one yellow	4 points
One yellow, one blue	5 points
Two yellows	6 points

Keep throwing the dice and adding to your score each time until you decide to stop. If your total goes over 21 your score for this turn is zero. If your score is less than 21, record it on your score card and hand the dice to the next player.

Continue in this way until one of you reaches 100.

Closer to 1000

This is a game for several players. Each player needs a score card. You will also need a calculator.

Each player should aim to get as close to 1000 as possible.

- Choose a starting number between 10 and 30.
- Multiply that number by a number between 1 and 10.
- Multiply that answer by another number between 1 and 10.

Compare your answers.

You score like this:

- The player closest to 1000 but not over 1000 scores 5 points.
- Other players with totals over 900 score 2 points.
- If your total is over 1000, you lose 2 points.

Play the game lots of times. How close to 1000 can you get?

Getting closer

Making connections

Connecting straws

Make some three-dimensional shapes by joining straws together.

Try shapes with 3 straws at each corner, or 4 straws, or ...

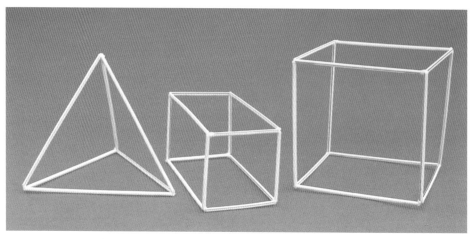

You could try a mixture of 3 straws at some corners and 4 straws at other corners.

▲ Crossing bridges

The city of Königsberg has two islands and seven bridges. A sketch map of the city looks like this:

The people of Königsberg wondered if they could walk around the city using every bridge just once. They thought they couldn't do it unless they built another bridge.

Do you agree with them? Why? If you think they need another bridge, where do you think they should build it?

Connecting numbers

This machine uses the rule multiply by 7 and add 2 to connect numbers.

Take turns to make up a rule and act as the machine.
The others give the 'machine' numbers and make a note of what the 'machine' turns the numbers into. Go on until someone guesses the rule.

Joining hands

Shake hands with everyone in your group.

How many handshakes were there?

How many handshakes would there be if someone else joined the group? And another person?

How many handshakes would there be for a group of 10 people?

● Connecting strips

Find six geostrips of the same length. Straws would do as well—
you could join them with modelling clay.

How many different two-dimensional shapes can you make with
them?

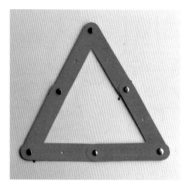 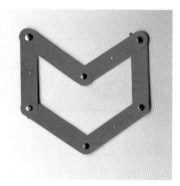 

Find out the names of the shapes you have made and write a
description of each one, saying as much as you can about it.

Swap your descriptions with others and see if you can draw their
shape by following their descriptions. Can you add anything to
make the description clearer or better?

If you choose a different number of geostrips to start with, can you
make more shapes?

Connecting squares

Groups of six squares that are joined together by whole sides only are called hexominoes.

These are hexominoes:

These are not:

Make a collection of hexominoes, using squares or squared paper. How many different ones have you found?

A cube has six square faces. Will all your hexominoes fold up to make a cube?

Make a group poster to show what you have done and try to explain why you can or cannot make a cube with your different hexominoes.

Find some plastic or card squares and equilateral triangles.

What different three-dimensional shapes can you make with them?

Display your shapes in two ways: show them flattened out to see how they started and show the finished three-dimensional shape.

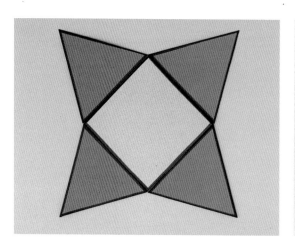
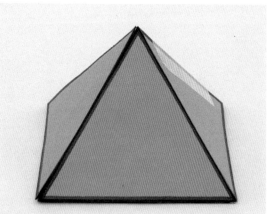

Choose another two-dimensional shape. Use it together with either your squares or your triangles to make a different set of three-dimensional shapes.

Compare your two sets of three-dimensional shapes. What stays the same? What changes?

Joining dots

Draw two dots on a piece of paper.

Take turns to join them with a line. The lines can be straight or curved, but they must not cross other lines.

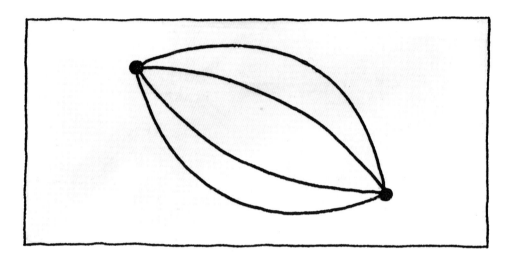

When you have all drawn a line, record the total number of lines drawn and the number of separate spaces you have made. Don't forget to count the space outside, as well.

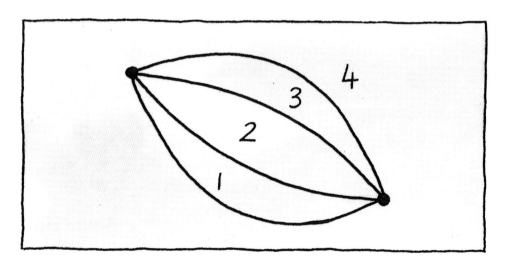

Now try with 3 dots, 4 dots and so on. Look for a pattern in the number of dots, number of lines and number of spaces.

This is a map of an underground system:

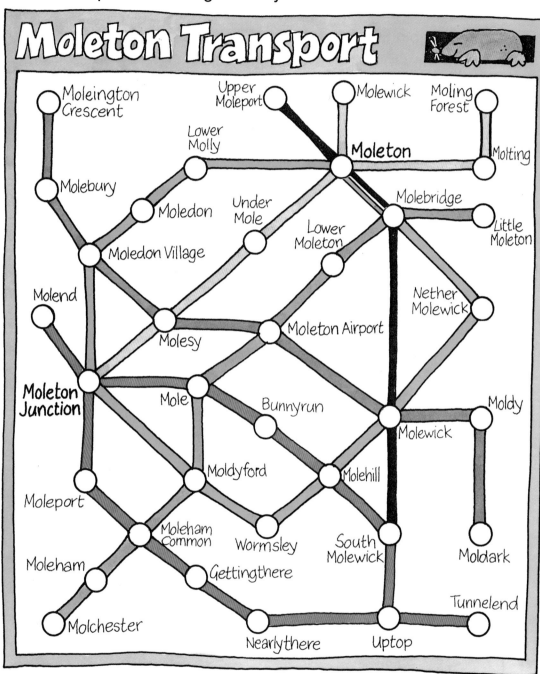

At some stations you can change from one line to another. Which stations connect the greatest number of lines?

Choose one of these stations. Re-draw the map so that your chosen station is in the centre.

Colouring maps

This is a map of Africa showing different countries.

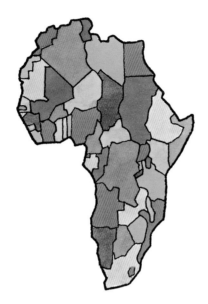

The artist has used seven colours to colour in this map. Can you use fewer colours but still make sure that no next-door countries are the same colour?

Make up some maps of imaginary countries and see what is the smallest number of colours you need for them, using the same rule.

Recording connections

Find different ways of recording the pairs of numbers that you used in **Connecting numbers**.

Ben chose this way to record them:

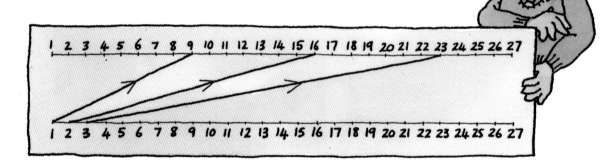

Tracey tabulated them:

Rahzic drew a graph:

Connecting Points

This is a game for up to four players. You will need a 6 x 6 grid and two dice. Each player should have about 20 counters of the same colour, with a different colour for each person.

Take turns to throw the dice and use the numbers to decide where to place a counter. You can choose which number represents a move along the grid: ⟹
and which represents a move up the grid: ⇧ .

Write down the coordinates of the points you used.

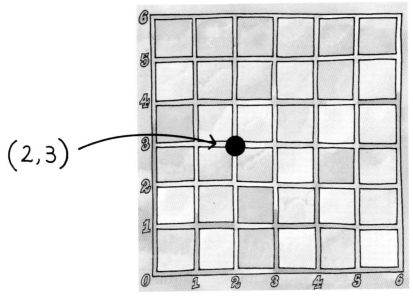

The aim is to get as many counters in a line as you can, but you may want to stop others getting lines as well. Continue until you have all placed all your counters, or until there are no points left to cover.

Score 3 for 3 counters in a line, 4 for 4 counters in a line and so on.

Look at one of your winning lines. You can score 5 extra points if you can find a pattern in the coordinates of the points on the line and describe it accurately to the others.

Happy and sad numbers

7 is a happy number,
because if you square it and then square each of the digits in the new number:

then add these two numbers together:

and keep squaring and adding like this:

you eventually end up with 1.

7	
↓	
49	$16 + 81$
↓	
97	$81 + 49$
↓	
130	$1 + 9 + 0$
↓	
10	$1 + 0$
↓	
1	

So it makes a pattern like this:

230 is happy too. Try it!

3 is a sad number. Its pattern looks like this:

Is 85 happy or sad?

In the world of numbers, are there more happy or more sad numbers? See what you can find out.

Joining points

How many joins are needed to connect the red dots to the green dots?

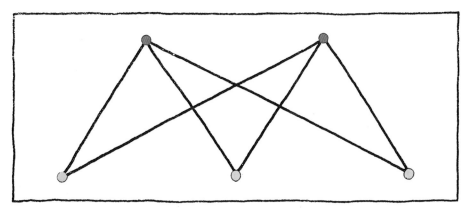

How many would be needed for 4 green dots? or for 5?
Explain how to work out how many joins are needed if you keep the same number of red dots but have different numbers of green dots.

Now look at the blue crossing points:

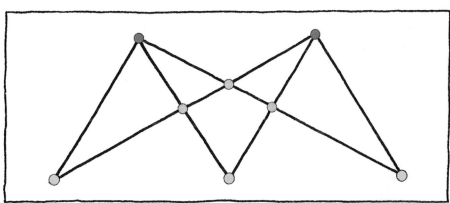

How many crossing points would there be for 4 green dots? for 10 green dots?

Make a table and use it to predict how many crossing points you will get for different numbers of green dots.

Can you work out a rule?

Green dots	Crossing places
2	1
3	3
4	

Triangular pyramids

Find a collections of marbles, spherical beads or balls.

Arrange them in triangles. Sometimes this is easier if you use modelling clay or make a frame to stop them rolling.

Build up some three-dimensional shapes like pyramids.

How many marbles are there in each shape?

How many would there be in the 5th shape? in the 6th shape?

How many would you need for the 10th shape?

Can you predict how many marbles would be in any shape?

Triangular number squares

+	1	3	6	10	15
1	2	4	7	11	16
3	4	6	9	13	18
6	7	9	12	16	21
10	11	13	16	20	25
15	16	18	21	25	30

What patterns can you find in this addition table?
Can you find any square numbers? or any triangular numbers?

Extend the table up to the first ten triangular numbers.

Make another table with triangular numbers, using −, x or ÷.

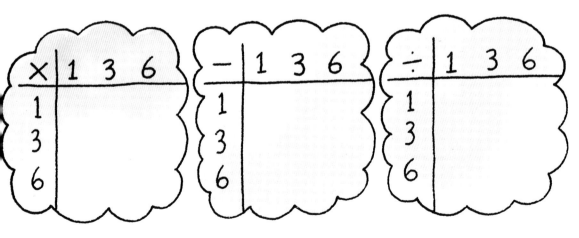

×	1	3	6
1			
3			
6			

−	1	3	6
1			
3			
6			

÷	1	3	6
1			
3			
6			

What patterns can you find?

Build a bridge

Maths at work

The give-away?

Collect some examples like
these of your own.

Is there a genuine saving?

Think up a good buy of your own. Make a poster to advertise why it
is a good buy.

Make a ramp

Find somewhere around your school that needs a ramp for
wheelchairs to use.

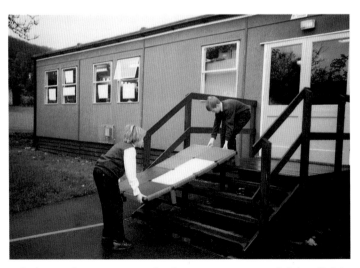

Make a model to show exactly how you would build it.
Explain how you built the model.

Patchwork patterns

Choose a patchwork pattern:

one of these

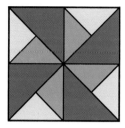 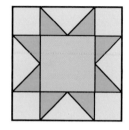

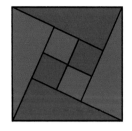 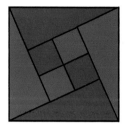

or these two together

Make a patchwork design by joining together several copies of your chosen pattern.

Find out what you can about the shapes in the patterns you made.

Selling comics or magazines

What makes people prefer one comic to another? What makes a magazine popular?

Write a report on some of your comics and magazines showing what makes them popular.

Which do you think is the best buy? Why?
Which would your family buy? Why?
Explain your family's choice to someone else.

Choose another product you like.

Compare sizes and prices and then say which you would buy
and why.

Where do you shop?

Is it cheaper to shop at the supermarket?
What extra costs might be involved in getting to the supermarket?

Choose an everyday item you buy regularly. What is the range of prices in your shops?

Which shops would you recommend and why?

Expensive potatoes?

What price per kilogram are the potatoes in packets of crisps?
How will you work it out?
What other costs are involved in making packets of crisps?

How much more expensive are potatoes as crisps than as frozen chips? as baking potatoes? as new potatoes?

More slopes

Make models to show what these signs mean.

Make a slope that goes 1 unit up for 4 units along the slope.

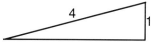

Make a slope that goes 1 unit up for 4 units along horizontally.

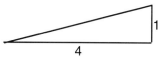

Compare the two slopes by rolling something down them. What do you notice?

Find out how far the Tower of Pisa leans.

How far can you make a set of identical boxes lean?

Egyptian triangles

Have you ever wondered how people in Ancient Egypt built pyramids?

They used triangles with sides of length 3, 4 and 5 units to make right angles for use in building.

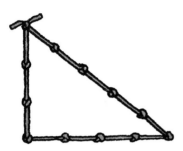

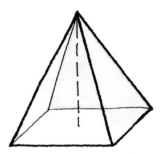

Make an Egyptian rope triangle. Use it to check some right angles. How accurate can you make it?

Make more 'Egyptian ropes' to decide which of the following will make right-angled triangles.

8,9,10 7,24,25 6,8,10

8,10,12 5,12,13 3,4,6

Can you find some more right-angled triangles?

How high?

Work out the height of some part of your school building.

Here are the heights of some famous buildings:

Big Ben.................................	97 m
St Paul's Cathedral	111 m
Canary Wharf Tower............	244m

Estimate how many times taller Big Ben is than your school. How about the other two buildings?

Use a clinometer to find out the height of some buildings near your school.

Add the information to your class sky-line.

Each of these three patchwork patterns uses a 'diamond' shape:

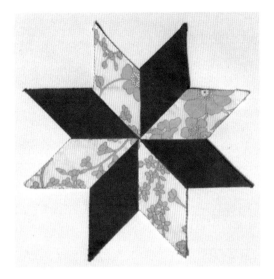

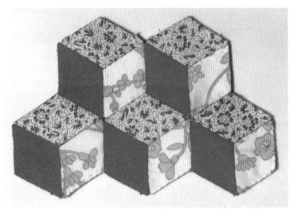

What is the same about each 'diamond' shape?
What is different?

Find out what you can about the angles and the sizes of the shapes used in the patterns. What are their correct names?

Make some patterns like them and experiment with the effects you can get by colouring them in different ways.

Frieze patterns

Look at these border patterns:

Experiment with some other border patterns.

Choose one to border a page or a picture.
How will you draw it accurately?

Use LOGO to draw a border pattern.

To go around the page or picture your pattern must turn corners.
Decide how you are going to do this.

Squares and circles

How many different patterns can you make using squares with coloured quarter circles, like these?

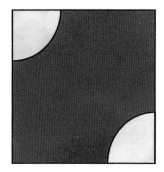 

You will need to make several copies of each.

Now try with these:

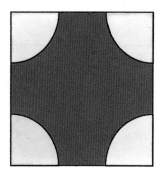 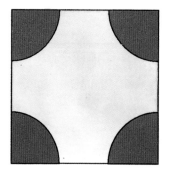

Patchwork makers arrange them to make patterns called 'Jockey Cap', 'Snowball', 'Queen's Crown' and 'Drunkard's Path'.

Make the arrangements that you think would have these names, or make up your own names for them.

How much?

How much do comics or magazines cost?

Which ones do you think are the best value for money?
How will you decide? Does everyone agree?

Make up an advertisement for the comic or magazine
you would choose as the best buy.

How would you convince other customers
that your choice is good value?

Colour supplements

Colour supplements come free with newspapers.

Choose a colour supplement to study.

How much space is taken up by advertisements?

What about the amount of space taken up by photographs?

What else could you find out?

How will you display your results?

	adverts	writing
Sunday News	2 sq. m.	3 sq. m.
The Reporter	2 sq. m.	2 sq. m.
The Weekly Star		
Daily Scoop		

percentage of advertisements

The Reporter	42%
Daily Scoop	30%
Sunday News	

Choose a newspaper and work out the weight of a 24-page supplement.

Kim delivers 20 papers. What extra weight will the delivery of 24-page supplements add?

If a delivery person is allowed to carry a maximum weight of 6 kg, will your chosen paper and its supplement be a problem?

What about a different newspaper?

A maths at work display